PRAYING WITH THE HEBREW SCRIPTURES

God's Surprising Presence

PRAYING WITH THE HEBREW SCRIPTURES

God's Surprising Presence

by
Maureena Fritz, NDS

SAINT MARY'S PRESS
CHRISTIAN BROTHERS PUBLICATIONS
WINONA, MINNESOTA

Acknowledgments

I am pleased to acknowledge my gratitude to the following people: Jack Rudin, whose curiosity and integrity build networks that draw together strength with strength, and gifts with needs, for the well-being of many people; Edward Arrigoni, whose support of scholarship in interfaith dialog is a commitment to peace with justice; Jack Driscoll, CFC, whose dedication to a vision of scholarship with pedagogy empowers many to teach and learn in loving and mutual respect; and Christiane Karmann, a young scholar pursuing a PhD in Christian and Jewish studies at the Ratisbonne Center in Jerusalem and the University of Saint Michael's College in Toronto. She did the designs in this book and brought to them her deep knowledge of Judaism and her love of art forms.

The acknowledgments continue on page 92.

The publishing team for this book included Carl Koch, FSC, development editor; Amy Schlumpf Manion, manuscript editor and typesetter; Christiane Karmann, illustrator; cover design by McCormick Creative/ Scott Chase; cover photo by Vernon Sigl; pre-press, printing, and binding by the graphics division of Saint Mary's Press.

Copyright © 1992 by Saint Mary's Press, 702 Terrace Heights, Winona, MN 55987-1320. All rights reserved. No part of this book may be reproduced by any means without the written permission of the publisher.

Printed in the United States of America

Printing: 6 5 4 3 2 1

Year: 1998 97 96 95 94 93 92

ISBN 0-88489-253-0

To Bro. Pierre Lenhardt, NDS

My brother and my rabbi never told me what I should do: he allowed me to share in his doing until I was able to begin doing myself. My doing now is an act of recognition of the power of his example. In thanksgiving, I dedicate this act of my doing to him.

> The world is charged with the grandeur of God.
> It will flame out, like shining from shook foil.
>
> Gerard Manley Hopkins, "God's Grandeur"

> Where I wander—you!
> Where I ponder—You!
> Only You, You again, always You!
> You! You! You!
> When I am gladdened—You!
> When I am saddened—You!
> Only You, You again, always You!
> You! You! You!
> Sky is You! Earth is You!
> You above! You below!
> In every trend, at every end,
> Only You, You again, always You!
> You! You! You!
>
> Martin Buber, *Tales of the Hasidim: The Early Masters*

Contents

Introduction 9

Meditations
   1. Where does God dwell? 15
   2. Where is God in patient suffering? 21
   3. Where is God in impatient suffering? 27
   4. Where is the place of God in our slavery? . . . 35
   5. Considering my wrongdoing, where is God? . . 41
   6. Does God dwell with me? 47
   7. Where does God speak? 55
   8. Where is the place of God in the Scriptures? . . 63
   9. How does God dwell in my soul? 71
 10. Where is the place of God's spirit? 79
 11. Where is God's place in our dying? 85

For Further Reading 90

Introduction

Where?

Our heart is restless until we find God. We seek God's presence, but where do we encounter the Divine? Each of these meditations asks the question *where*. Where are you, God? Where are you in creation? Where are you in death?

Asking these questions and finding the answers can put us on a path to holiness.

A Book of Prayer

This is a book of prayer. The readings, the commentaries, and the reflections following each commentary are designed to help you enter into prayer. Although you may find many of the ideas in this book thought-provoking, the intent of the book is to lead you into communication with God.

The Use of the Scriptures and Jewish Sources

The readings are taken from the Old Testament, more properly called the Hebrew Scriptures, and from other collections of ancient Jewish prayers.

Because the Hebrew Scriptures, also called the "Torah," have their roots in the Jewish community, I have turned to the Jewish religious tradition for help in understanding and explaining certain passages. In recent years, most Christian denominations have reminded their members that God spoke and continues to speak through the Jewish people. These are the people whom God chose to receive the divine revelation at Sinai and whose mission it is to give the Torah to the world.

If we hope to understand Jesus, we must try to understand what it means to be Jewish. Jesus was Jewish, as were his parents, his relatives, and most of his original disciples. In an address to Catholic bishops gathered from around the world in March

1982, Pope John Paul II commented: "Our common spiritual heritage [with Jews] is considerable. Help in better understanding certain aspects of the church's life can be gained by taking an inventory of that heritage, and also by taking into account the faith and religious life of the Jewish people as professed and lived now as well" (Eugene J. Fisher, *Seminary Education and Christian-Jewish Relations: A Curriculum and Resource Handbook,* app. D).

You will notice that throughout this book, I have consistently used the word *Torah* for God's word. *Torah* is a dynamic Hebrew word that means more than "God's word." It also means studying, praying, and living out that word. As you start each meditation, keep in mind that traditional Judaism and Christianity teach that praying, studying, and living the word cannot be separated. When we study God's word, we are praying. When we live out God's word by acting justly, lovingly, and peacefully, we are still praying.

Except for the quoted prayers and scriptural passages, I have used inclusive language. When you are reading the quoted passages from the Torah or from the Jewish *Daily Prayer Book* that use exclusive language, you may wish to change the masculine pronouns to plural pronouns. The word *Torah* itself is a feminine word form in the Hebrew language.

Suggestions for Using the Meditations

The Illustrations: Aids to Prayer

An illustration using Hebrew words introduces each meditation. At first the strange lines may mean little to you. After reflecting on the art, however, you will realize that the design captures the essence of the meditation. You may also find that the illustration remains with you long after you have put the book aside. So begin each prayer session by meditating on the illustration.

Some clarifications might aid your reflection on the illustrations.

This sign ה, a Hebrew letter pronounced "hay," always stands for God. Wherever you see this letter, you should see the presence of God in the design. The artist has taken certain liberties in drawing this letter, so it may take the shape of a vine or a house. Try to discover this letter when you ponder each illustration. The presence of God takes many forms for us; so does this letter ה in the illustrations. Other Hebrew letters compose the rest of each illustration. The English translation of these letters is given, too.

Notice the light and dark shadings in the illustrations. The light emanates from God's presence. Where darkness forms in the illustrations, look for the light that penetrates or hovers over the gloom. The Hebrew of the Bible is considered to be a holy language. Light is said to shine from the Hebrew letters, even if one does not recognize or know how to pronounce them.

In addition, strong, firm lettering denotes strength and security. Weak, tentative letters indicate hesitancy and timidity.

Finally, ponder the overall design formed by the letters. Ask yourself what the design means.

Divine Study

Slowly read through each meditation from beginning to end. Although the Torah readings could yield a lifetime of meditation, the commentary directs you to reflect on one theme. To do this, I have explained a few points most important to that theme.

Slow reading and studying of the scriptural passage and the commentary will aid your understanding and, as has been pointed out, is a form of praying. Studying holy texts has been compared to the action of a winepress. When we read, we put the reading into our mouth as a grape is put into a winepress. Our heart seeks to understand the "grape." To do so, read and study until one point strikes you or begins to stand out in your mind.

If you need a more structured approach to doing holy study, or *lectio divina,* you might use this process:

1. Relax yourself in God's presence. Breathe deeply and slowly. Offer simple prayers of faith, thanksgiving, and praise.
2. Slowly read the passage aloud, keeping the theme of the meditation clearly in focus. Ponder any word or line that seems to attract you. Repeat the word or line slowly over and over again, letting its significance become clear.
3. Read the passage aloud again. This time respond with a prayer to God based on the word or line that you find most significant.

4. Read the passage once more. Reflect on this question: How does this word touch my life at this particular time?
5. Close with the Lord's Prayer.

The Reflections

Each meditation offers several ways of reflecting on the reading. Select just one of the reflection activities that draws you into further conversation with God about the aspect of the text most significant to you. Save the other points for reflection for another prayer period.

Recall the grape in the winepress. As you meditate, a process also called *meditatio,* you are beginning to press the "grape," drawing the juice from it that will ferment into wine. The holy text, like a grape in a winepress, must be pressed by your heart if it is to turn into vintage wine.

Your reflection may require simple waiting. Good wine takes time. Be patient. Some wines take longer to ferment than others.

Oratio: **One of the Fruits of Meditation**

Prayer, or *oratio,* lets your heart speak and sing, celebrating the grapes pressed during divine study and the wine fermented during meditation. God's presence should be proclaimed.

Some of the meditations invite you to sing, hum, or even whistle hymns praising God. You may respond by simply repeating the memory verse all through your day. Or spontaneous words of praise may be another fitting response to God's abundant mercy.

Contemplation

Some of the prayer periods may result in contemplation; that is being silently present or attentive to the loving God. In contemplation, you let go of your intent, your agenda, your action. Instead, you become filled with God-light, God-present. This is God's precious gift. It cannot be purchased or gained through one's own efforts.

Sharing with a Prayer Partner

Using this book to pray with a partner may be enriching. Consider inviting someone to share this experience.

Here is a process that you might follow when praying with another person:

1. Consider the illustration together. Try to gain an understanding by pondering it, sharing insights, and then reading the explanation.
2. After a careful, meditative reading of the scriptural passage and the commentary, use the process of divine study, *lectio divina,* outlined previously. At each stage, share the response indicated.
3. Choose one of the reflection activities. Spend some quiet time in meditation, and then come together to share your reflections.
4. End your shared prayer by reciting the memory verse, singing a hymn, or offering praise and thanks to God with a formal or spontaneous prayer.

My hope is that you will discover or rediscover God's holy presence in all the times and places of your life. Blessed be God's name.

אָכֵן יֵשׁ יְהוָה בַּמָּקוֹם הַזֶּה וְאָנֹכִי לֹא יָדָעְתִּי׃

"Surely the LORD is in this place—and I did not know it!"

(Genesis 28:16)

The Hebrew letter ה, pronounced "hay," stands for "the LORD," and is shaped like a strongly built house. Within the walls of the LORD's house, we rest secure. God dwells with and cares for us, and so the Hebrew letters inside the ה read, "Surely the LORD is in this place!" Since we do not always see the house—the LORD—the arms of ה are not totally blackened. And, when we fail to recognize that we reside in the LORD's house, we can become prostrate before our fear like the timid letters that read, "and I did not know it."

MEDITATION 1

Where does God dwell?
In every place, even the most unlikely, "'Surely the LORD is in this place—and I did not know it!'" (Genesis 28:16).

Introduction

Our heart is restless for God. Like parched land thirsts for water, we long for God. But where do we find God? Through the Hebrew Scriptures, we know that God lives in the very place where we are standing, no matter how delightful or awful that spot may be.

Reading

> Jacob left Beer-sheba and went toward Haran. He came to a certain place and stayed there for the night, because the sun had set. Taking one of the stones of the place, he put it under his head and lay down in that place. And he dreamed that there was a ladder set up on the earth, the top of it reaching to heaven; and the angels of God were ascending and descending on it. And the LORD stood beside him and said, "I am the LORD, the God of Abraham your father and the God of Isaac; the land on which you lie I will give to you and to your offspring; and your offspring shall be like the dust of the earth, and you shall spread abroad to the west and to the east and to the north and to the south; and all the families of the earth shall be blessed in you and in your offspring. Know that I am with you and will keep you wherever you go, and will bring you back to this land; for I will not leave you until I have done what I have promised you."

Then Jacob woke from his sleep and said, "Surely the LORD is in this place—and I did not know it!" And he was afraid, and said, "How awesome is this place! This is none other than the house of God, and this is the gate of heaven." (Genesis 28:10–17)

Commentary

In this biblical narrative, Jacob sets out to escape the wrath of his brother Esau and to look for a wife in the land from which his mother came. As night draws near, he lies down in a barren and stony spot under the open sky. While sleeping, he has a dream that changes him from a person unaware of God to one who suddenly knows that God is with him.

This narrative bears rich meaning. Jacob registers his response to the dream-vision by initially exclaiming, "'Surely the LORD is in this place—and I did not know it!'" Then, as he trembles with fear and wonder, he adds, "'How awesome is this place!'" Amazingly, a place that just a few hours before seemed a heap of stones on a barren landscape suddenly becomes the house of God and the gate of heaven.

God's most intimate name LORD is repeated several times in the passage. God introduces the Divine Self: "'I am the LORD.'" By this name, God chooses to stand by Jacob, and it is the name by which Jacob first comes to know God as he exclaims, "'Surely the LORD is in this place!'" This name is so important because it is specifically used to indicate the generous mercy and tenderness of God (Exodus 34:6). So when God says, "'I am with you and will keep you wherever you go,'" we, like Jacob, can rest secure.

Another striking element in this passage is the number of times the word *place* (*maquom* in Hebrew) is repeated: five times in seven short verses. *Place* or *maquom* is another name for God. So when Jacob declares, "'How awesome is this place!'" in effect he is saying, "How awesome is God!" Thus, the place on which he is standing is no longer just any place but one filled with the presence of God. God is *in* the place, and God *is* the place on which Jacob is standing. Later, Moses chooses the name *Bethel* for this spot where Jacob stood because it means "house of God."

Three elements—a place, the Divine Presence, and wonder—are all aspects of an encounter between God and us. God may be encountered in any and every place. The Divine Presence permeating all places at all times makes a Divine-human encounter possible. And finally, our wonder invites encounter. Indeed, without wonder we cannot encounter God even though we are standing in the place of God's presence. Wonder is both the condition and the result of the presence of the Divine. In wonder, we may cry out, "'Surely the LORD is in this place—and I did not know it!'" What the Divine reveals depends on God's will for us and our ability to receive the revelation. Jacob was able to encounter the tender, loving side of God.

Reflection

❏ After reading the introduction, the reading from Genesis, and the commentary, use the process of *lectio divina* outlined below:
1. Relax yourself in God's presence. Breathe deeply and slowly. Offer simple prayers of faith, thanksgiving, and praise.
2. Slowly read the passage aloud, keeping the theme of the meditation clearly in focus. Ponder any word or line that seems to attract you. Repeat the word or line slowly over and over again, letting its significance become clear.
3. Read the passage aloud again. This time respond with a prayer to God based on the word or line that you find most significant.
4. Read the passage once more. Reflect on this question: How does this word touch my life at this particular time?
5. Close with the Lord's Prayer.

❏ Look around you, right where you are. Ponder each object in the place; caress each thing with your eyes. Close your eyes and listen; let each sound record itself in your mind. Smell whatever scents permeate the place. Repeat this process of awareness, slowly praying: "'Surely the LORD is in this place!'" (Genesis 28:16).

❏ Recall a time when your spiritual journey took you through a barren wilderness. Maybe you lost a loved one, or a relationship fell apart, or you experienced a devastating failure. Did you experience God's presence during or after the desert time? If you did feel God's presence, how did you experience God? Talk with

God about the time. If God seemed absent and you felt abandoned, talk to God about the absence, what you may have learned from the experience, and your own reluctance to invite God into your place of wilderness.

❑ Invite images of your present life to flood your consciousness. Let the images flow by like a motion picture, with barren spots and lush pastures alike. In what images do you find God present? In what places do you miss God's presence? Thank God for the times you sense the Divine Presence, and then ask God to be with you in the barren spots, too. Then pray over and over meditatively: This _____ [mention your barren spot] is none other than the house of God, and this is the gate of heaven.

❑ Try to recall a significant dream from your sleep, or bring to mind a personal dream you strive to create. Reflect on what the aspects of the dream mean for you and what emotions you feel during the dream. Remember that God can reveal the divine self in both light and dark images or feelings. Cherish the dream; wonder at it. Invite God to tell you the importance of your dream. Then pray repeatedly God's words to Jacob: "'Know that I am with you and will keep you wherever you go'" (Genesis 28:15).

❑ After you have calmed your body by stretching and relaxing all of your muscles and breathing deeply, close your eyes and bring to mind a favorite place—a place where you easily find God's presence. In your memory, give your senses freedom to take in the whole scene including all the fragrances, sights, sounds, and feelings. Thank God for this place of refuge. Bask in God's presence and God's words, "'I will not leave you'" (Genesis 28:15). Sing, hum, or whistle your favorite hymn of thanksgiving.

Memory Verse

Take this verse with you in your heart and on your lips:

> "Surely the LORD is in this place—and I did not know it!"
> (Genesis 28:16)

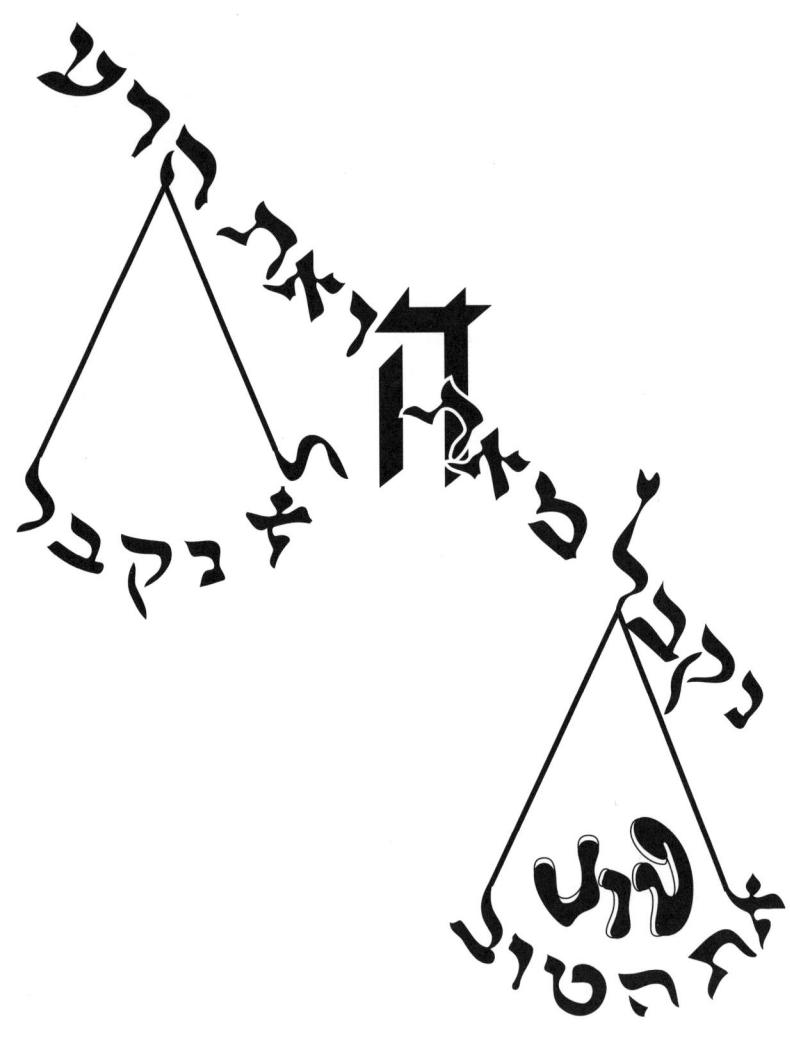

אֶת־הַטּוֹב נְקַבֵּל מֵאֵת הָאֱלֹהִים וְאֶת־הָרָע לֹא נְקַבֵּל

"Shall we receive the good at the hand of God, and not receive the bad?"

(Job 2:10)

If there is weight on only one side of a scale, it is not balanced. If we receive only good things from God, our life loses its movement, tension, and dynamism. Appreciating goodness becomes difficult in the absence of badness. When bad things happen, we realize what good means. By praising God in the midst of his suffering, Job puts movement back into the scale. The LORD, ה, is the one on whom our life hangs and balances. The LORD centers and supports us. Anchored in the LORD we are able to endure the winds of outrageous fortune.

MEDITATION 2

Where is God in patient suffering?

In acceptance of God's will, "'Shall we receive the good at the hand of God, and not receive the bad?'" (Job 2:10).

Introduction

The array of vicissitudes in life tests our belief in God's sovereignty and continuous presence. We may frequently fluctuate between faith and doubt, joy and sadness, hope and despair. At times, like Job, we heartily give thanks for God's protection in the midst of adversity. At other times, weakened by misfortune, we complain, Why does all this have to happen to me? Job's response to misfortune dramatizes these two contrasting sides of our personality. This meditation focuses on Job the Patient, and the next meditation on Job the Impatient.

Reading

> Then Job arose, tore his robe, shaved his head, and fell on the ground and worshiped. He said, "Naked I came from my mother's womb, and naked shall I return there; the LORD gave, and the LORD has taken away; blessed be the name of the LORD."
>
> In all this Job did not sin or charge God with wrongdoing. (Job 1:20–22)

Commentary

In this reading and in other parts of the Book of Job (the prologue; chapters 1; 2; 40:7–17; and the epilogue), we find Job the Patient.

The setting is pastoral. Job is a wealthy inhabitant of Uz. He has seven sons and three daughters. After the children's annual week of feasting, he offers the customary burnt offerings for all of them in order to make expiation for any sin they may have committed. An accuser, here called Satan, argues with God that piety coupled with wealth cannot be disinterested piety. Satan puts this challenge to God: Let the LORD try denying Job of his wealth, and Job will deny the LORD to the LORD's face.

Through a series of calamities, Job loses all of his property and his sons and daughters in a single day. Four successive messengers inform Job of these disasters. Upon hearing the message of the last one, Job performs the usual act of mourning (1:20), but a disparaging word about God never crosses his lips. On the contrary, he declares, "'Naked I came from my mother's womb, and naked shall I return there; the LORD gave, and the LORD has taken away; blessed be the name of the LORD.'"

Satan then argues with God that the true test of piety is bodily suffering. With God's permission, he strikes Job with a terrible inflammation that covers his skin from head to foot. Subsequently, Job squats in the ashes scratching himself with a shard. But still Job does not "sin with his lips" (2:10). On the contrary, to his wife's suggestion that he denounce the God who rewards his loyalty so shabbily, Job retorts indignantly, "'You speak as any foolish woman would speak. Shall we receive the good at the hand of God, and not receive the bad?'" (2:10).

Next, three of Job's friends, Eliphaz the Temanite, Bildad the Shuhite, and Zophar the Naamathite, on learning of Job's sufferings, come to comfort him (2:12–13). They urge Job to denounce God for allowing his suffering, but still Job holds fast to his integrity. Instead of denouncing God, he declares:

> "As God lives, who has taken away my right,
>   and the Almighty, who has made my soul bitter,
> as long as my breath is in me
>   and the spirit of God is in my nostrils,
> my lips will not speak falsehood,

> and my tongue will not utter deceit.
> Far be it from me to say that you are right;
> until I die I will not put away my integrity from me."
>
> (27:2–5)

These scenes from Job's story invite us to encounter a hero, a model of uncommon integrity tormented by the most extraordinary adversity. Blameless and upright, Job fears God and turns away from evil. He lives in right relationship with his family and community, and in harmony with himself. Although horrible misfortune strikes him, Job the Patient magnanimously accepts his fate as the expression of the Divine Will. Integrity meets adversity head on and defeats it.

In the epilogue, God affirms Job. In the space of two verses (42:7–8), God refers twice to "my servant Job" who speaks what is right. Put to a much crueler test than Abraham (Genesis chapter 22), Job proves that he is unconditionally a God-fearing person and that he believes we must remain patiently devoted to God under all circumstances.

Reflection

❏ Using the process of *lectio divina* (pages 11–12), pray the reading from Job 1:20–21 and review the commentary.

❏ In the extremities of his suffering, poor Job praised God's name and accepted God's will. What about "poor you"? What is the worst fate that could befall you? By using the power of your creative imagination, imagine the very worst catastrophe that could happen to you. Bring it to mind now; stay with the image. Try to imagine all the details of your worst fear realized.

Now ask yourself: In the midst of my worst fear, can I praise God's will, God's name? You may need help in answering this question. Do not be afraid to ask for God's help.

❏ Job's wife and friends urged him to curse God. Bring to mind people and occasions that have tempted you to curse God. How did you respond to God?

❏ You may wish to write down the names of people as you answer the following questions:
- Do I know of people who do not see or feel the pain and suffering in the world or in their own life?
- Do others numb themselves into a state of indifference to both joy and sorrow, and pride themselves on their stoicism?
- Do I know anyone who remains untouched by the whips and lashes of outrageous fortune?
- Do some display in their adult eyes the innocence of a child rather than the compassion that comes from life experience?

After you have recalled people for whom these characteristics apply, ask yourself if you agree with this statement from Thomas Gray:

> Where ignorance is bliss,
> 'Tis folly to be wise.

Even if you do not really agree with the statement, do you sometimes feel tempted to avoid hard decisions, conflicts, or suffering at all costs? Talk with God about this question.

Memory Verse

Each time you meet with frustration, hurt, or disappointment today, repeat these words:

> "Shall we receive the good at the hand of God, and not receive the bad?"
>
> (Job 2:10)

רבה ע.נ.י. ראתה

לישמיע לישמיע לישמיע אזן אזן אזן אזן אזן אזן אזן אזן ישמיעני

לְשֵׁמַע־אֹזֶן שְׁמַעְתִּיךָ וְעַתָּה עֵינִי רָאָתְךָ:

"I had heard of you by the hearing of the ear,
but now my eye sees you."

(Job 42:5)

Hearing of someone is not the same as seeing that person. Seeing seems more factual, clear, straight, and sharp, whereas uncertainty accompanies hearing. In the drawing, the sound waves composed of broken letters portray the uncertainty of hearing, as in, "'I had heard of you by the hearing of the ear.'" The string of strong letters in a straight vertical line proclaims, "but now my eye sees you." What was uncertain becomes real. The whole design forms the letter ה. God is known through the ear and through the eye; through hesitant searching and through clear insight. On the one hand, God is real, a fact to the believer; on the other hand, God is a mystery that can never be fully understood.

MEDITATION 3

Where is God in impatient suffering?

In honesty and trust, "'I had heard of you by the hearing of the ear, / but now my eye sees you'" (Job 42:5).

Introduction

We become who we are through the process of living. Spiritual growth takes place when, through our suffering, we become less rebellious toward the universe, less frightened of the future, and more sympathetic to those around us. Yet to become like Job the Patient takes a lifetime of experiences. Many of us never learn such acceptance. Before Job could utter, "'the LORD gave, and the LORD has taken away; blessed be the name of the LORD'" (1:21), he underwent sufferings and trials far greater than those of Abraham. In the process of becoming Job the Patient, he was first Job the Impatient, then Job the Blasphemer, the Doubter, the Frenzied Rebel, and God's Challenger who, in the end, casts himself down in utter humiliation and repents in dust and ashes.

Reading

> "Why is light given to one in misery,
>   and life to the bitter in soul,
> who long for death, but it does not come,
>   and dig for it more than for hidden treasures.
> Therefore I will not restrain my mouth;
>   I will speak in the anguish of my spirit;
>   I will complain in the bitterness of my soul.
> I loathe my life;
> I will give free utterance to my complaint;

> I will speak in the bitterness of my soul.
> Let me have silence, and I will speak,
> and let come on me what may."
>
> (Job 3:20–21; 7:11; 10:1; 13:13)

Commentary

The Book of Job opens with the statement that Job was blameless and upright, and that he feared God and turned away from evil. In a day, through no fault of his own, Job loses everything: his property and possessions, all of his children, and his own health. The same Job who blesses the divine name of God and holds fast to his integrity also curses his own life in the face of seeming injustice. Moreover, he accuses God of the most dreadful atrocities. In the end, God responds to him and Job learns a timeless lesson.

While Job admits that, as a human being, he is not pure in comparison with God (14:1–6) and even confesses that he may have committed some misdeeds in the time of his youth (13:26), he knows that his sufferings are all out of proportion to his misdeeds. Consequently, Job shouts that God attacks him "'without cause'" (9:17). Because Job does not doubt for an instant that God is directly responsible for his plight, he accuses God of behaving like the following:

A capricious tyrant:

> "Though I am innocent, I cannot answer him;
>   I must appeal for mercy to my accuser.
> If I summoned him and he answered me,
>   I do not believe that he would listen to my voice.
> For he crushes me with a tempest,
>   and multiplies my wounds without cause;
> he will not let me get my breath,
>   but fills me with bitterness."
>
> (9:15–17)

A corrupt judge:

> "Though I am innocent, my own mouth would condemn me;
>   though I am blameless, he would prove me perverse."
>
> (9:20)

A wild beast that devours his flesh:

> "He has torn me in his wrath, and hated me;
> > he has gnashed his teeth at me;
> > my adversary sharpens his eyes against me."
>
> (16:9)

A ruthless warrior:

> "I was at ease, and he broke me in two;
> > he seized me by the neck and dashed me to pieces;
> he set me up as his target;
> > his archers surround me.
> He slashes open my kidneys, and shows no mercy;
> > he pours out my gall on the ground.
> He bursts upon me . . . like a warrior."
>
> (16:12–14)

A murderer:

> "See, he will kill me; I have no hope."
>
> (13:15)

One who will not listen to an appeal:

> "If I wash myself with soap
> > and cleanse my hands with lye,
> yet you will plunge me into filth."
>
> (9:30–31)

Confused in mind and heart, Job condemns the perceived injustice of God and yet expects to receive an acquittal from God:

> "Oh, that I knew where I might find him,
> > that I might come even to his dwelling!
> I would lay my case before him,
> > and fill my mouth with arguments.
> > And I should be acquitted forever by my judge."
>
> (23:3–4,7)

Job desperately seeks the presence of a God who eludes his pursuit:

"If I go forward, he is not there;
  or backward, I cannot perceive him;
on the left he hides, and I cannot behold him;
  I turn to the right, but I cannot see him."

(23:8–9)

Job also senses that God is searching for him, but will not find him:

"Why do you not pardon my transgression
  and take away my iniquity?
For now I shall lie in the earth;
  you will seek me, but I shall not be."

(7:21)

Although Job seeks God, the presence of God overwhelms him more completely than the darkness of his impending death:

"I am terrified at his presence;
  when I consider, I am in dread of him.
God has made my heart faint;
  the Almighty has terrified me;
If only I could vanish in darkness,
  and thick darkness would cover my face!"

(23:15–17)

Crushed by the enormity of his plight and confusion, Job pleads, "'Let the Almighty answer me!'" (31:35). This is Job's final challenge to God.

The Almighty replies from out of a whirlwind and in an unusual manner. God asks questions instead of giving direct answers, and through these questions Job realizes that he understands little about the mysteries of the universe. If Job cannot understand these mysteries, how can he understand the problem of evil or the suffering of innocents?

The Book of Job ends not with the hero's accusations and annihilation, but with God's appearance to Job and its effect upon him. Job repents in dust and ashes and acknowledges God's presence:

"Therefore I have uttered what I did not understand,
  things too wonderful for me, which I did not know.
I had heard of you by the hearing of the ear,

> but now my eye sees you;
> therefore I despise myself,
> and repent in dust and ashes."
>
> (42:3,5–6)

These are the last words of Job the Impatient. If God consents to reveal the Divine Self to human beings and instruct them, who should question God's providence and concern for the world? Job the Impatient no longer attempts to completely comprehend the scheme of things because he has not only heard but also seen.

Reflection

❏ Focusing on the theme of the meditation, pray the words of Job again. Follow the pattern of *lectio divina:* relax; read the passage aloud and ponder a significant line or phrase; read it again and pray with the line; read the passage once more and then meditate on the message of the passage for you; end with the Lord's Prayer.

❏ Job the Patient accepts his condition, but Job the Impatient accuses God of abandoning him. In John's Gospel, Jesus the Lamb of God dies, declaring simply, "'It is finished'" (19:30). In Mark's Gospel, Jesus cries out from the cross: "'My God, my God, why have you forsaken me?'" (15:34). Reflect on the parallels between Job's and Jesus' acceptance of God's will and their feelings of abandonment. How do these different reactions parallel your own response to crisis and suffering?

These cries of anguish fundamentally express the desire to reach out to God. Have there been times in your life when you have accused God of abandoning you? When you made your complaint to God, did you realize that God stood with you all along?

❏ Job's agony wavers incessantly between denial and affirmation, doubt and certainty, revolt and acceptance, despair and hope. List some issues in your life that cause you to fluctuate in a similar manner, for example, troubled relationships or physical suffering. Compose a prayer of lamentation to God and then offer the Almighty your complaint as Job does. If you fear God's anger, recall that God knows your heart anyway. Naming your complaints demonstrates your trust in God's care and can help you identify your own situation.

❑ In the presence of the most holy God, all of Job's pain is alleviated. Job becomes aware of his sinfulness at the very instant of his reconciliation, and he is saved at the moment of his surrender. Recall a time when you became reconciled with another person or with God. Bring to mind the emotions that you felt.

Now examine your soul. Like Job, name the sin in your life and offer it to God; for instance, name your sin, and then pray: In the sorrow for this sin, I seek your mercy, God, and acknowledge my dependence on you.

Memory Verse

Whenever you grow impatient or weary of the foibles of other people today, pray:

> "I had heard of you by the hearing of the ear,
>   but now my eye sees you."
>
> (Job 42:5)

הַמָּקוֹם אֲשֶׁר אַתָּה עוֹמֵד עָלָיו אַדְמַת־קֹדֶשׁ הוּא:

"The place on which you are standing is holy ground."

(Exodus 3:5)

The letter ה, God's presence, is lying flat on the ground. God's presence rests in every place on the earth. Across the earth, covered with the letter ה, are the words, "The place on which you are standing is holy ground." All of the letters, including the ground-covering ה, are transparent, indicating the shining holiness of every place on which you stand.

MEDITATION 4

Where is the place of God in our slavery?

In God's sharing of our suffering, "'The place on which you are standing is holy ground'" (Exodus 3:5).

Introduction

In our last two meditations, we reflected on human suffering. This meditation focuses on the suffering of God. How does God feel when humans suffer? God suffers with us. Like parents who agonize over their child's suffering, wishing they could assume the burden of the child's pain, so does God agonize and suffer. Just as the parents' joy is limited when their child is in pain, so too is God's joy limited when God's people are afflicted.

Reading

> Moses was keeping the flock of his father-in-law Jethro, the priest of Midian; he led his flock beyond the wilderness, and came to Horeb, the mountain of God. There the angel of the LORD appeared to him in a flame of fire out of a bush; he looked, and the bush was blazing, yet it was not consumed. Then Moses said, "I must turn aside and look at this great sight, and see why the bush is not burned up." When the LORD saw that he had turned aside to see, God called to him out of the bush, "Moses, Moses!" And he said, "Here I am." Then he said, "Come no closer! Remove the sandals from your feet, for the place on which you are standing is holy ground." He said further, "I am the God of your father, the God of Abraham, the God of Isaac, and the God of Jacob." And Moses hid his face, for he was afraid to look at God. (Exodus 3:1–6)

Commentary

This passage reminds us that all places are holy ground because God's presence permeates the world. But the passage expresses much more. Two powerful images of God and the relationship of the people of Israel to God dominate this passage: fire and the lowly bush.

Midrashic lore—traditional exposition of biblical texts by Jewish scholars—explains that the bush is one of the lowliest trees in the land, compared with the lofty cedars of Lebanon. Its branches are stubby, knotted, tough, and covered with thorns that point downward. Dust and sand from the desert cloak it. Biting desert winds and burning rays of the sun are its rough companions. So lowly is the shrub that the Scriptures do not even bother to give it a name.

In the reading, fire envelops the shrub. The flame and the bush are so entwined that distinguishing one from the other is futile. Yet, in this passage, the fire does not consume the bush, nor does it die out.

The fire and the lowly bush symbolize the relationship between God and enslaved Israel. God identifies the Divine Self with Israel. God (the flame) and Israel (the bush) are entwined together. What happens to one, happens to the other; the situation of one is the situation of the other. The Exodus story occurs at the point in the history of the Jews when Israel was enslaved by Egypt, groaning under the heavy hand of the pharaoh.

Israel is not alone. God is telling the people that the Divine Presence will remain with them in their lowliness and suffering. Because of love, God not only dwells with people in their suffering but shares in their suffering as well.

God communicates this message to the Israelites, not in a thundering voice from atop the mountain of Sinai, but rather "out of a bush," that is, from among the thorns. When Moses stops to look at the strange sight, he sees God peering at him through the thorns. In the oral Torah—the living tradition that interprets the written Torah or the Scriptures—God says to Moses: "'Do you not realise that I live in trouble just as Israel live[s] in trouble? Know from the place whence I speak unto you—from a thorn-bush—that I am, as it were, a partner in their trouble'" (H. Freedman and Maurice Simon, trans., *The Midrash Rabbah*, vol. 2, p. 53).

The bush (Israel) holds the flame (God) the way a thornbush entraps a bird. Once the bird enters a thornbush, which has needles pointing downward, it cannot escape without being torn to shreds. Likewise, as the flame and the bush cannot be separated from each other, God and Israel cannot be separated. They are, so to speak, twins. The oral Torah surmises that like one twin who feels the other's headache, so it is with the Holy One: "I will be with them in trouble" (Psalm 91:15).

But God and Israel are more than partners. God is present to the Israelites as a community and to each member individually. God reassures each Israelite that the pain she feels, God feels; that what he endures, God endures. Like the individual, God suffers, is enslaved, and is rebuffed. When an Israelite has a headache, God also has a headache.

Out of love, God chooses to suffer with people and be enslaved with them. God also chooses to let the Divine Self be redeemed. When the Israelites are redeemed, God will be redeemed!

Reflection

❑ Review the theme of the meditation, and then pray with the reading from Exodus, using the process of divine study, or *lectio divina*.

❑ Light a candle or several candles. Or, if you have a fireplace, you might light a fire. Then, while looking at the fire, calm yourself. Relax your body by stretching all parts of it from your feet to your head. Breathe deeply and slowly, over and over, remembering that this is a holy place and that God dwells even in the life-giving air. While gazing at the flames, imagine the scene that Moses saw, the bush inflamed. Hear God say to you, I am a partner in your pain! Aloud and slowly, repeat God's words.

If you wish, write down any reflections and feelings that occur in this meditation.

❑ Moses' experience of a suffering God changed his mission. As Moses worked to liberate the Hebrew slaves, he also liberated God, the divine self. Moses had not only an earthly mission but a cosmic one.

In this light, meditate on these questions:
- How do I act, even in small ways, to liberate my sisters and brothers from oppression?
- Do I recognize that God cannot be separated from poor and needy people? If I serve God's people, I serve God. If I oppress God's people, I oppress God.
- From what slavery, addiction, area of ignorance, or destructive habit do I need liberation?

Converse with God about any one or all of these questions, seeking light and strength from your partner.

❏ Moses turned aside from his work to look at the great sight of the burning bush. Are there any great sights that you pass by in your daily life? As you travel to work or run errands, look closely around you. Notice the great sights. Try to look at people today. How are they great sights to you? Record in writing all of the great sights you see, and then offer a prayer of thanksgiving to God who offers these great sights.

Memory Verse

As you enter each different place today—the kitchen, the car, the office, wherever—pray:

> "The place on which you are standing is holy ground."
> (Exodus 3:5)

הַשֹּׁכֵן אִתָּם בְּתוֹךְ טֻמְאֹתָם

[God's presence] remains with them in the midst of their uncleannesses.

(Leviticus 16:16)

"God remains with them in the midst of their uncleannesses" is written in dark letters to represent "uncleannesses." Yet these strong, dark letters have a light side, showing that God is still present to sinners even in their corruption. God's presence casts a protective and challenging shadow over the ground of uncleanness.

MEDITATION 5

Considering my wrongdoing, where is God?

In the very place of my sin, "[God's presence] remains with them in the midst of their uncleannesses" (Leviticus 16:16).

Introduction

We are unable to flee from God, for our very being is rooted and grounded in God. Even when we sin, God is present. God's presence manifests itself in the discomfort we feel when we sin and in our determination to repent of and forsake our sin.

Reading

> David's son Absalom had a beautiful sister whose name was Tamar; and David's son Amnon fell in love with her. Amnon was so tormented that he made himself ill because of his sister Tamar, for she was a virgin and it seemed impossible to Amnon to do anything to her. But Amnon had a friend whose name was Jonadab . . . and Jonadab was a very crafty man. . . . Jonadab said to him, "Lie down on your bed, and pretend to be ill; and when your father comes to see you, say to him, 'Let my sister Tamar come and give me something to eat.' . . . So Amnon lay down, and pretended to be ill; and when the king came to see him, Amnon said to the king, "Please let my sister Tamar come and make a couple of cakes in my sight, so that I may eat from her hand."
>
> Then David sent home to Tamar, saying, "Go to your brother Amnon's house, and prepare food for him." So

Tamar went to her brother Amnon's house. . . . Amnon said, "Send out everyone from me." . . . He took hold of her, and said to her, "Come, lie with me, my sister." She answered him "No, my brother, do not force me; for such a thing is not done in Israel; do not do anything so vile! As for me, where could I carry my shame? And as for you, you would be as one of the scoundrels in Israel." . . . But he would not listen to her; and being stronger than she, he forced her and lay with her.

Then Amnon was seized with a very great loathing for her; indeed, his loathing was even greater than the lust he had felt for her. Amnon said to her, "Get out!" . . . He called the young man who served him and said, "Put this woman out of my presence, and bolt the door after her." (2 Samuel 13:1–17)

Commentary

When God and humanity live together, contentment and calm rarely result. In fact, the situation that is created may be more paradox than paradise because a person's primitive instincts battle with her or his divine aspirations.

In the struggle, a sinner actually experiences the dis-ease, pain, and nausea of sin. Amnon is a case in point. Amnon's heinous sin turns his obsession for Tamar into a loathing far stronger than the overwhelming attraction he had originally felt for her. Tragically, he transfers his self-hatred for the abomination he has committed onto the humiliated and innocent Tamar. Not satisfied with telling her to get out, Amnon commands his servant boy, "'Put this woman out of my presence, and bolt the door after her.'" He can no longer even form her name on his lips, but refers to her as "this woman."

God is present to Amnon in the dis-ease, defilement, self-loathing, and self-hatred caused by sin. His loathing for the sin could have compelled him to pray and ask forgiveness. Indeed, his father, David, was stricken to the heart because of his many sins. He repented and became reconciled to God: "'I have sinned greatly in what I have done. But now, O LORD, I pray you, take away the guilt of your servant'" (2 Samuel 24:10).

Instead of admitting his sin and letting God into his heart, Amnon heaps his loathing on Tamar. We have no record that Amnon repented, only that Absalom murders him to avenge Tamar's rape. Had Amnon repented, both he and Tamar could have experienced healing.

Actually, two paths to repentance lie open to the sinner. One path is revealed through shock and the feelings of horror at what one has done. The second path to repentance is found through the intellectual realization of the destructiveness of one's deeds and the accompanying change of heart. Whether the process of repentance begins in the heart or the mind, the impulse to convert comes from one's interior Guest, the Most Holy God who dwells within the temple of the soul.

Reflection

❑ Prayerfully study the passage from 2 Samuel, keeping the theme of the meditation clearly in focus.

❑ Bring to mind several of your worst sins, whether from the recent or the distant past. Then recall in as much detail as possible all aspects of each sin and all of the accompanying emotions. Ponder each of the following questions:
- Did I transfer any of my guilt and self-loathing onto anyone else?
- Did I try to rationalize my sinfulness?
- What were the effects of my sin on other people, on the physical or moral environment, and on myself?
- What emotions, reasons, or other influences moved me to repentance?
- Did I see God's helping hand in my repentance?

❑ These words were revealed by God to Moses on Mount Sinai. Repeat them slowly several times:

> "The LORD, the LORD,
> a God merciful and gracious,
> slow to anger,
> and abounding in steadfast love and faithfulness,

keeping steadfast love for the thousandth generation, forgiving iniquity and transgression and sin."

(Exodus 34:6–7)

When a person sins, a distance is created between the sinner and God, as it is written,

> Your iniquities have been barriers
> between you and your God.

(Isaiah 59:2)

But if God left the sinner completely, who would create dis-ease within the sinner—those first movements of discomfort that urge the sinner to repent?

Sinners remove themselves from God's presence, but God remains with them, calling them to return. When sinners repent, they reunite themselves with God.

Now pray the passage from Exodus again. Each time you pray the words, bring to mind a different transgression for which you have yet to be reconciled to God or a moral dilemma facing you. Invite God into your repentance and your decision-making process.

❏ Using the process of *lectio divina*, meditate on the story of the prodigal son, Luke 15:11–32.

❏ Are there people with whom you need to be reconciled, people you offended or abused? Talk with God about practical steps that you could take to seek forgiveness and to make amends.

Memory Verse

Recall any sin you may have committed today and pray this verse:

> [God's presence] remains with them in the midst of their uncleannesses.

(Leviticus 16:16)

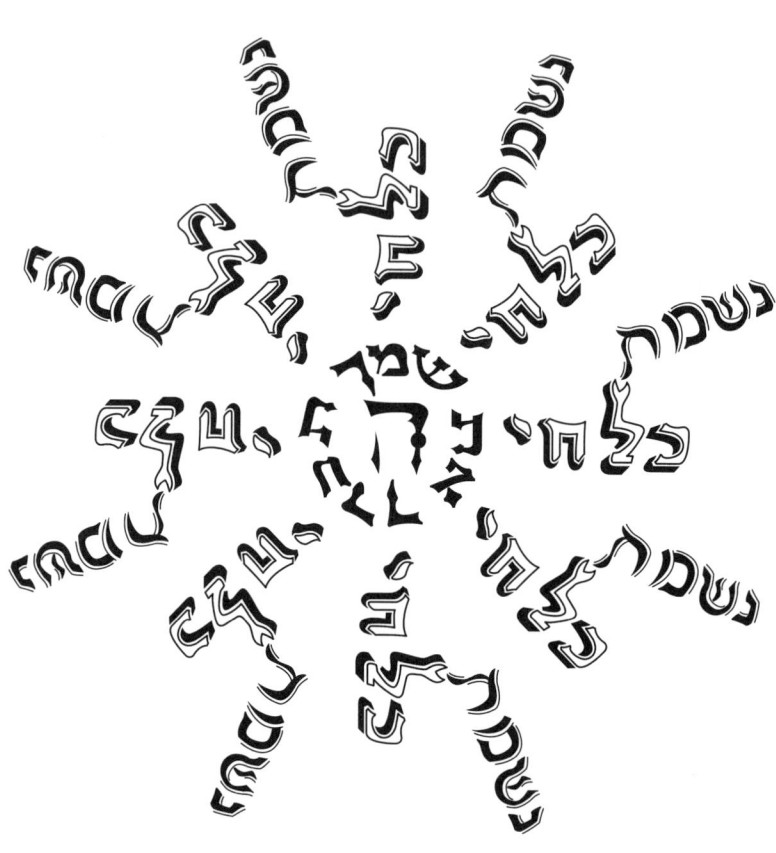

נִשְׁמַת כָּל חַי תְּבָרֵךְ אֶת־שִׁמְךָ יְיָ אֱלֹהֵינוּ

The soul of every living being shall bless thy name, Lord our God.
(Philip Birnbaum, trans.,
Prayer Book for Sabbath and Festivals, p. 148)

God, in the shape of the Hebrew letter ה, as the center of the sun, sends out rays of light into the world. And, conversely, everything comes to the center, toward God. Three different types of lettering are used in this design. The letters in the center are strong and dark. As we get closer to the center (God), strength is gained but so is a sense of mystery. Some of the letters surrounding the center are predominantly shadowed with some light, while others are almost wholly light with traces of shadow. The spirits of all people contain both light and dark. But whatever the variation, the soul of every living creature blesses God's holy name.

MEDITATION 6

Does God dwell with me?

Yes, in the sanctification of God's name, "The soul of every living being shall bless thy name, Lord our God" (Birnbaum, *Prayer Book for Sabbath and Festivals*, p. 148).

Introduction

In Middle Eastern culture, a name is not merely a label but a reality. To know a name is to know the person or object being specified. If the name dwells in a place, the object named also dwells there. When the Divine Name dwells in a place, God dwells there in person. We see this when God tells the Israelites, "then you shall bring everything that I command you to the place that the LORD your God will choose as a dwelling for his name" (Deuteronomy 12:11). Not only does God cause the Divine Name to dwell in a place, but God has given us the power to cause the Name, the Divine Presence, to dwell in a place.

Reading

> In the year that King Uzziah died, I saw the Lord sitting on a throne, high and lofty; and the hem of his robe filled the temple. Seraphs were in attendance above him; each had six wings: with two they covered their faces, and with two they covered their feet, and with two they flew. And one called to another and said:
>
> > "Holy, holy, holy is the LORD of hosts;
> > the whole earth is full of his glory."

The pivots on the thresholds shook at the voices of those who called, and the house filled with smoke. And I said: "Woe is me! I am lost, for I am a man of unclean lips, and I live among a people of unclean lips; yet my eyes have seen the King, the LORD of hosts!"

Then one of the seraphs flew to me, holding a live coal that had been taken from the altar with a pair of tongs. The seraph touched my mouth with it and said: "Now that this has touched your lips, your guilt has departed and your sin is blotted out." Then I heard the voice of the Lord saying, "Whom shall I send, and who will go for us?" And I said, "Here am I; send me!" And he said, "Go." (Isaiah 6:1–9)

Commentary

Like Isaiah, we sanctify the Name and cause it to dwell on the earth in three different ways: prayer, exemplary conduct, and martyrdom.

Prayer: We sanctify God's name and acknowledge God's presence through prayer by making the song of the angels our own,

"Holy, holy, holy is the LORD of hosts;
the whole earth is full of his glory."

Our words of proclamation have the power to do what they proclaim, to fill the world with God's glory.

When a community declares, in the traditional Jewish Kedushah prayer, "We sanctify thy name in this world even as they sanctify it in the highest heavens," God's name is hallowed. Further along, when the prayer announces,

"The Lord shall reign forever,
Your God, O Zion, for all generations,"

those praying help to establish God's Reign. Finally, convinced of the power of the word to sanctify the Name, the community promises: "Through all generations we will declare thy greatness; to all eternity we will proclaim thy holiness; thy praise, our God, shall never depart from our mouth, for thou art a great and holy

God and King. Blessed art thou, O Lord, holy God. Thou art holy and thy name is holy, and holy beings praise thee daily. Blessed art thou, O Lord, holy God" (Philip Birnbaum, trans., *Daily Prayer Book: Ha-Siddur Ha-Shalem,* pp. 84, 86). Whenever we invoke the Ineffable Name, we invoke the presence of God and bless God's power and might.

Exemplary conduct: The second way to sanctify God's name is through ethical conduct. When Isaiah says, "Here am I; send me!" in effect, he asks God to set him on the path of right action. Ethical conduct means walking in the ways of God (Deuteronomy 10:12). Just as God is

> "merciful and gracious,
> slow to anger,
> and abounding in steadfast love and faithfulness,
> keeping steadfast love for the thousandth generation,
> forgiving iniquity and transgression and sin,"

so also are we to be merciful, patient, loving, faithful, and forgiving (Exodus 34:6). As God clothes the naked (Genesis 3:21), so are we to clothe the naked. As God comforts mourners (Genesis 25:11), so are we to comfort mourners. And, as God buries the dead (Deuteronomy 34:6), so are we to bury the dead.

Unethical acts are called *hillul Ha-Shem,* meaning "desecration of the Name." Someone who cheats, steals, or maligns a neighbor ravishes the glory of God. God's honor is tied to the acts of God's creatures. In Isaiah 43:10, God says,

> "You are my witnesses . . .
>   whom I have chosen,
> so that you may know and believe."

When we act rightly, we give witness to God's presence. When we sin, we desecrate God's name.

Martyrdom: God's name is hallowed by all conduct that urges people to honor their God. The Holy Name is *supremely* hallowed when people lay down their life rather than abandon their religion or violate the law of God. The example of the mother and her seven sons (2 Maccabees 7:1–42) and the story of Shadrach, Meshach, and Abednego in the fiery furnace (Daniel, chapter 3) serve as models of conduct in the sanctification of the

Name. A believer should be willing to die rather than desecrate the Name.

Through these three ways—prayer, exemplary conduct, and martyrdom—we sanctify God's name and cause God's presence to be installed in the place of sanctification.

Reflection

❑ Meditate on the reading from Isaiah, using the process of *lectio divina*.

❑ Biblical names express some important quality of the person: *Tamar* means "palm tree"; *Daniel* means "God judges"; *Hannah* comes from a word meaning "graciousness." Simon's name is changed to *kēphas*, or *Peter*, from the words for *rock* in Aramaic (*kêphā*) and Greek (*petra*), respectively. *Jesus* is a Hebrew word meaning "salvation."
Does your name express something of who you are? Have you ever thought of giving yourself a name that expresses a central quality of yourself?

❑ Praising or calling upon God's name was important to Jesus. You may wish to reflect on these passages: Luke 11:2, John 5:43, or John 12:28.

❑ The following prayer is known as the Kaddish. Compare this to the Lord's Prayer. Notice how both prayers begin by hallowing the Name and continue by praying for the establishment of God's Reign. Pray the Kaddish slowly and reverently:

> Glorified and sanctified be God's great name, throughout the world which he has created according to his will. May he establish his kingdom in your lifetime and during your days, and within the life of the entire house of Israel, speedily and soon; and say, Amen.
> May his great name be blessed forever and to all eternity.
> Blessed and praised, glorified and exalted, extolled and honored, adored and lauded be the name of the Holy One,

blessed be he, beyond all the blessings and hymns, praises and consolations that are ever spoken in the world; and say, Amen. (Birnbaum, *Daily Prayer Book,* p. 50)

❏ Review your life of prayer, using these questions:
- Do I give witness to God's presence by praying to God's name in public?
- How often do I pray?
- Do I often praise and thank God for all of God's wonders, or do I mostly pray when I need something from God?
- Do I pray "big," that is, do I trust God enough to discuss the central topics in my life or to ask for my major needs?

❏ When God called to him, Isaiah responded, "'Here am I; send me!'" (Isaiah 6:8). How have you told God, Here am I; send me! when God has asked the following questions:
- Have you been merciful?
- Do you respond patiently?
- How are you reflecting my love to people?
- Have you forgiven those who have harmed you?
- Have you clothed the naked, visited the sick, comforted the mourners, and buried the dead?

❏ Even though you may not be called to die in God's name, you may be called to sacrifice in other ways for the sake of God's Reign: for instance, you may have to intervene to get treatment for an alcoholic friend, or you may have to discipline your children when you would prefer to give in. Meditate on ways in which you have been called to martyrdom and, as you remember each small death, pray with Saint Ignatius of Loyola: "Take, Lord, and receive. . . . Give me only your love" (David L. Fleming, trans., *The Spiritual Exercises of St. Ignatius,* p. 141).

❏ Go visit a friend, a person who you know would welcome your company or a person who is grieving. If you cannot make a visit, write this person a letter. In either case, pray the person's name to God.

❏ A simple prayer is the repetition of one of the divine names. Sit quietly for a while. As you breathe in, recite the name of Jesus or another sacred name; recite the holy name again as you exhale. Try this way of praying.

Memory Verse

Every time you hear your own name called today, pray this verse:

> The soul of every living being shall bless thy name, Lord our God.
> (Birnbaum, *Prayer Book for Sabbath and Festivals,* p. 148)

קָרוֹב אֵלֶיךָ הַדָּבָר מְאֹד

The word is very near to you.

(Deuteronomy 30:14)

The text, in the form of a Torah scroll, reads: "This commandment that I am commanding you today is not too hard for you, nor is it too far away. It is not in heaven. . . . Neither is it beyond the sea. . . . The word is very near to you" (Deuteronomy 30:11–14). Note the Hebrew letter ה, the symbol of God, in the midst of the scroll. God can be seen through the Hebrew letters and words of the Torah, which are like the garments of God. The letters reflect the different variations of light and dark found in the Scriptures. But through them all, God can be found by the diligent searcher. The handles of the Torah scroll are written in strong, firm letters indicating that the word is not abstract, but definite and concrete. The letters that form the handles of the scroll read: "The word is very near to you."

MEDITATION 7

Where does God speak?
In the Torah, "The word is very near to you" (Deuteronomy 30:14).

Introduction

We can find God in the Torah. Just as the body and soul dwell together, so does God dwell in the word as a garment that both conceals and reveals. We need not ask, "'Who will go up to heaven for us, and get it for us so that we may hear it and observe it?'" (Deuteronomy 30:12). This revealing and concealing word can be found very near—in our mouth and in our heart.

Reading

> Surely, this commandment that I am commanding you today is not too hard for you, nor is it too far away. It is not in heaven, that you should say, "Who will go up to heaven for us, and get it for us so that we may hear it and observe it?" Neither is it beyond the sea, that you should say, "Who will cross to the other side of the sea for us, and get it for us so that we may hear it and observe it?" No, the word is very near to you; it is in your mouth and in your heart for you to observe. (Deuteronomy 30:11–14)

Commentary

God is present in the great revelation of the written Torah—the Scriptures; and in the oral Torah—the instructions and legal opinions about the written Torah contained in works like the *Mishnah, Midrash, Tosafot,* and so on.

Trying to separate God, the Divine Self, from the content of revelation contained in the Scriptures can be tempting. But we must be careful not to do this. The Torah is not something outside God, and God is not outside the Torah. God is present in the divine word, not detached from it.

The image of a garment expresses the relationship between God and the Torah. A garment reveals and conceals. A garment reveals by bringing out the beauty and the form of the person. But a garment can also conceal parts of the body or the whole body, including the face. The material must be drawn aside to see the beauty of the face hidden underneath. Likewise, the Torah both reveals and conceals the Divine Face:

> David thus said: "Open thou mine eyes, that I may behold wondrous things out of thy law" (Ps. 119:18), to wit, the things that are beneath the garment. Observe this. The garments worn by a man are the most visible part of him, and senseless people looking at the man do not seem to see more in him than the garments. But in truth the pride of the garments is the body of the man, and the pride of the body is the soul. Similarly the Torah has a body made up of the precepts of the Torah, called *gufe torah* (bodies, main principles of the Torah), and that body is enveloped in garments made up of worldly narrations. The senseless people only see the garment, the mere narrations; those who are somewhat wiser penetrate as far as the body. But the really wise, the servants of the most high King, those who stood on Mount Sinai, penetrate right through to the soul, the root principle of all, namely, to the real Torah. (Maurice Simon and Harry Sperling, trans., *The Zohar,* vol. 5, p. 211)

In Hebrew, *Torah* is a feminine word form, and thus stands for the feminine face of God. She herself parts the drapes that conceal her, so that her followers may be attracted to her beauty. The following story illustrates how she attracts her lovers to deeper and deeper depths of understanding and knowledge:

> Thus the Torah reveals herself momentarily in love to her lovers in order to awaken fresh love in them. Now this is the way of the Torah. At first, when she begins to reveal herself

to a man, she makes signs to him. Should he understand, well and good, but if not, then she sends for him and calls him "simpleton", saying to her messengers: "Tell that simpleton to come here and converse with me", as it is written: "Whoso is a simpleton let him turn in hither" (Prov. 9:4). When he comes to her she begins to speak to him, first from behind the curtain which she has spread for him about her words suitable to his mode of understanding, so that he may progress little by little. This is called *"Derasha"* (Talmudic casuistry, namely the derivation of the traditional laws and usages from the letter of Scripture). Then she speaks to him from behind a thin veil of a finger mesh, discoursing riddles and parables—which go by the name of Haggadah. When at last he is familiar with her she shows herself to him face to face and converses with him concerning all her hidden mysteries and all the mysterious ways which have been secreted in her heart from time immemorial. Then such a man is . . . a true adept in the Torah, a "master of the house", since she has revealed to him all her mysteries, withholding and hiding nothing. (Harry Sperling, Maurice Simon, and Paul P. Levertoff, trans., *The Zohar,* vol. 3, pp. 301–302)

God dwells in the Torah, beckoning us, luring us, calling us into God's divine and loving presence. The more time we spend with the word of God, the nearer we come to God, the more enlightened we become, and the more of life we enjoy.

Reflection

❑ Using the steps of *lectio divina,* pray the reading from Deuteronomy. Write your reflections about this passage.

❑ List some of your favorite passages from the Scriptures, passages that reveal yet also conceal the mystery of God or that touch some deep place within you. To aid you in this process, recall the time, place, and circumstances when you last read this passage. For instance, maybe at a point of transition in your life you doubted God's existence. Then you might have read the story about Jesus curing the boy possessed by an evil spirit. The words, "'All things can be done for the one who believes'" (Mark 9:23) may have lifted your soul to pray for faith.

Next, perhaps over several days, pray with each passage. Let God be present to you in the word.

❑ Slowly pray these verses from Psalm 19:7–10. Pray the psalm over and over again, letting the voice of God into your heart:

> The law of the LORD is perfect,
>   reviving the soul;
> the decrees of the LORD are sure,
>   making wise the simple;
> the precepts of the LORD are right,
>   rejoicing the heart;
> the commandment of the LORD is clear,
>   enlightening the eyes;
> the fear of the LORD is pure,
>   enduring forever;
> the ordinances of the LORD are true
>   and righteous altogether.
> More to be desired are they than gold,
>   even much fine gold;
> sweeter also than honey,
>   and drippings of the honeycomb.

Then pose these questions to yourself for meditation:
- How have the Scriptures revived my soul?
- How have the Scriptures been like a revealing and concealing garment of God?
- Has my heart rejoiced when God's word has been revealed?
- Have the Scriptures lured me to love God and my neighbor more fervently?
- How do I taste the sweetness of living according to God's law?

❑ The First Psalm says:

> Happy are those
>   who . . .
> delight . . . in the law [the Torah] of the LORD,
>   and on his law [the Torah] they meditate day and night.
> They are like trees
>   planted by streams of water,

> which yield their fruit in its season,
>   and their leaves do not wither.
> In all that they do, they prosper.

(Vv. 1–3)

How do you dwell in the place of God in the Torah? Do you need to spend more time with it? Is there a friend or a group with whom you could share the Torah?

Memory Verse

Our words contain power. They affect those who hear them. This is even more true when we utter words from the Scriptures. Spiritual potencies and new lights are created. With this in mind, repeat slowly several times:

> The word is very near to you.

(Deuteronomy 30:14)

קָרוֹב אֵלֶיךָ הַדָּבָר מְאֹד בְּפִיךָ וּבִלְבָבְךָ לַעֲשֹׂתוֹ׃

The word is very near to you; it is in your mouth and in your heart for you to observe.
(Deuteronomy 30:14)

We find God by studying the Scriptures. The presence of God in the word is symbolized by the ה, which forms each page. The ה on the left page is a mirror image of the ה on the right page. Authentic study of the Torah bears fruit in the practice of the Torah. Hence the phrase "to observe it," לעשתו, becomes the bookmark that accompanies you through the whole Torah, page after page.

MEDITATION 8

Where is the place of God in the Scriptures?
In the study and observance of the Torah, "The word is very near to you; it is in your mouth and in your heart for you to observe" (Deuteronomy 30:14).

Introduction

We can find God in the study of the Torah, God's word. As we probe, study, and turn the word over and over again, we find wisdom, inspiration, and instruction, in addition to finding God. If ten people sit together and occupy themselves with the Torah, the presence of God is with them. Even if just one person studies the Torah, God is present. The secrets of the Torah reveal themselves only to those who labor in the Torah. But study of the Torah also includes observance of the Torah. The person who studies and observes the Torah becomes like a bubbling, fresh fountain that flows with never-ending life.

Reading

> Surely, this commandment that I am commanding you today is not too hard for you, nor is it too far away. It is not in heaven, that you should say, "Who will go up to heaven for us, and get it for us so that we may hear it and observe it?" Neither is it beyond the sea, that you should say, "Who will cross to the other side of the sea for us, and get it for us so that we may hear it and observe it?" No, the word is very near to you; it is in your mouth and in your heart for you to observe.
>
> See, I have set before you today life and prosperity, death and adversity. If you obey the commandments of the

LORD your God that I am commanding you today, by loving the LORD your God, walking in his ways, and observing his commandments, decrees, and ordinances, then you shall live and become numerous, and the LORD your God will bless you in the land that you are entering to possess. . . . I call heaven and earth to witness against you today that I have set before you life and death, blessings and curses. Choose life so that you and your descendants may live, loving the LORD your God, obeying him, and holding fast to him; for that means life to you and length of days. (Deuteronomy 30:11–20)

Commentary

Faced with a choice between life and death, who would not choose life? But how do we choose life? We obey the commandments of the LORD our God that are commanded, love the LORD our God, and walk in God's ways.

Two times in the first paragraph of the biblical text, we read, "that we may hear it and observe it," and when the word is in our mouth and in our heart, again the injunction is to observe it.

Hear and observe. Study of the Torah includes observance of the Torah. The phrase *Talmud Torah* includes aspects of both hearing and observing. *Talmud* is a dynamic Hebrew word that means learning by both study and action. Hence, *Talmud Torah* means both teaching and studying the Torah, and it also means the Torah itself as studied and taught. The first definition of *Talmud Torah* refers to an activity; the second to a result, the content of revelation.

Talmud Torah, as study of the Torah, is a serious matter, a matter of life and death. The following prayer, recited at least twice daily by devout Jewish people, proclaims a profound love for God and the Torah. The "merciful Father" is entreated to enlighten our eyes and minds to understand and to observe God's word.

> With a great love hast thou loved us, Lord our God; great and abundant mercy hast thou bestowed upon us. . . . Be gracious to us and teach us likewise. Our Father, merciful Father, thou who art ever compassionate, have pity on us and

> inspire us to understand and discern, to perceive, learn and teach, to observe, do, and fulfill gladly all the teachings of thy Torah. Enlighten our eyes in thy Torah; attach our heart to thy commandments; unite our heart to love and reverence thy name. . . . Thou hast chosen us from all peoples and nations, and hast forever brought us near to thy truly great name, that we may eagerly praise thee and acclaim thy Oneness. Blessed art thou, O Lord, who hast graciously chosen thy people Israel. (Birnbaum, *Daily Prayer Book*, pp. 74, 76)

This prayer reminds us that to be chosen for the sake of the Torah places a heavy responsibility on the elected people. But to be chosen is also a great honor and joy.

Rabbi Akiba lived during the Roman occupation of Israel when an order went out to the Jews not to study or teach the Torah. Despite this order, Akiba continued to study and teach until he suffered martyrdom by being flayed alive by the Romans. He compared *Talmud Torah* to living waters. Just as fish cannot leave the streams without suffocating, neither could he think of leaving his study of God's word. His love demanded knowledge of God, and his knowledge of God demanded study of the Torah.

Talmud Torah as a way to God and a way to build God's Reign on earth equals in importance all other ways to God and ways to transform the world:

> These are things whose fruits a man enjoys in this world while the capital is laid up for him in the world to come: honouring father and mother, deeds of loving-kindness, making peace between a man and his fellow; [but] the study of the Law is equal to them all. (Herbert Danby, trans., *The Mishnah*, pp. 10–11)

The Torah is equal to them all because from Torah study comes knowledge and love of God that is expressed in love of neighbor and good deeds.

Hence, if disaster comes to a nation, it is because the nation neglected *Talmud Torah:*

> Why is the land ruined and laid waste like a wilderness. . . ? And the LORD says: Because they have forsaken my law that

I set before them, and have not obeyed my voice, or walked in accordance with it, but have stubbornly followed their own hearts. (Jeremiah 9:12–14)

With *Talmud Torah* as the center of the community and the center of one's days, life abounds. That is the meaning of God's commandment:

Choose life so that you and your descendants may live, loving the LORD your God, obeying him, and holding fast to him; for that means life to you and length of days, so that you may live in the land that the LORD swore to give to your ancestors. (Deuteronomy 30:19–20)

Reflection

❑ Prayerfully study the reading from Deuteronomy.

❑ Ponder this phrase: So that you may hear it and observe it. What are the different ways you can hear and observe the word?

❑ Meditate on the prayer from the *Daily Prayer Book* cited in the commentary.

❑ In meditation 7, the reflection on pages 56–57 asked you to list some of the passages from the Scriptures that are most important to you. Return to this list of passages. Study each one. Review its message for you and ask yourself how you "observe" the teaching of the passage.

❑ To study the Torah means to spend time pondering God's word—chewing it, tasting it, and allowing oneself to be influenced and moved by it. Do you devote a part of each day or each week to the study of God's word? Is God giving you an inclination or a nudge to walk in this direction?

❑ "No, the word is very near to you; it is in your mouth and in your heart for you to observe" (Deuteronomy 30:14). Sometime during the coming week, reflect on these words with a friend, remembering that "'where two or three are gathered in my name, I am there among them'" (Matthew 18:20).

❏ Pray these words from Proverbs:

> My child, if you accept my words
>   and treasure up my commandments within you,
> making your ear attentive to wisdom
>   and inclining your heart to understanding;
> if you indeed cry out for insight,
>   and raise your voice for understanding;
> if you seek . . .
>   for it as for hidden treasures—
> then you will understand the fear of the LORD
>   and find the knowledge of God.
>
>   (2:1–5)

Then, study the parable of the sower who went out to sow seed (Mark 4:1–20).

Memory Verse

On the hour today, silently pray:

> The word is very near to you; it is in your mouth and in your heart for you to observe.
>
>   (Deuteronomy 30:14)

וְאַתֶּם הַדְּבֵקִים בַּיהוָה אֱלֹהֵיכֶם חַיִּים כֻּלְּכֶם הַיּוֹם׃

Those of you who held fast to the Lord your God are all alive today.

(Deuteronomy 4:4)

The elongated ה forms the stalk of a vine. The vine wraps itself around the stalk, its life. As the vine clings to and crawls up the stalk, it receives more life and more energy, which the curling branches represent: "Those of you who held fast to the Lord your God are all alive today."

MEDITATION 9

How does God dwell in my soul?

By my soul cleaving to God, "Those of you who held fast to the LORD your God are all alive today" (Deuteronomy 4:4).

Introduction

In the last meditation, we contemplated the Torah as the milieu of God's presence and noted the example of Rabbi Akiba who refused to give up the study and teaching of the Torah even to the point of death. The Torah was the "life element" (*hiyyut*) in which he lived. If the word is our *hiyyut*, then God is also our life element, or *hiyyut*. As Saint Paul said, "'"In him we live and move and have our being"'" (Acts 17:28). The soul within us has a center that is not simply where God wants to reside, but the place where God wants to lovingly communicate the Divine Self. As a result of this relationship, the Divine is implanted permanently within the human soul.

Reading

> Then God said, "Let us make humankind [*adam*] in our image, according to our likeness. . . . Then the LORD God formed man [*adam*] from the dust [*adamah*] of the ground, and breathed into his nostrils the breath of life; and the man [*adam*] became a living being [*nephesh hayyah*]. (Genesis 1:26; 2:7)

> Those of you who held fast to the LORD your God are all alive today. (Deuteronomy 4:4)

Choose life so that you and your descendents may live, loving the LORD your God, obeying him, and holding fast to him; for that means life to you. (Deuteronomy 30:19–20)

Commentary

God is present in all the aspects of our life: in the place on which we are standing, in our suffering, in our sin, in our blessing of God's name, in the words of the Torah, and in the holy of holies within our soul. Indeed, not only is God present in our soul, but God is part of our soul. One part of our soul is God from God, Light from Light, true God from true God.

Jewish and Christian tradition holds that the soul contains faculties of willing, thinking, and feeling. In the Scriptures, the following are five different expressions for the soul:

1. *Nephesh* (vitality): the lowest life force of the body, which even plants possess
2. *Ruah* (spirit): a higher spiritual faculty possessed even by the animals
3. *Neshamah* (soul): a divine force that vivifies the intellect
4. *Hayyah* (living): an even more refined spiritual level of the soul
5. *Yechida* (divine spark): the innermost point of the soul, united and one with God. *Yechida* is the divine spark itself that clothes the Divine.

The awesome mystery of God's intimate presence as the *yechida*, the innermost point of our soul, might better be understood by likening it to images in nature.

A tree planted in the ground: A tree's existence is rooted in the earth in which it is planted. The roots of the tree become entwined with the soil and receive nourishment and support from this soil for the whole tree. It is as though the branches and leaves are unaware of their dependence on the soil.

Our soul's existence is rooted in God: "Choose life . . . loving the LORD your God . . . holding fast to him; for that means life to you." Our divine soul cleaves to God and lives at one with God, even if we, like the branches and leaves of a tree, are not aware of it. Without this cleaving to God, the soul dies.

A chip of stone from a rock: Just as a sculptor hews a work of art from a slab of stone, so is the divine soul hewn from the rock that is God. Our divine soul shares the same essence of God. Isaiah says, "Look to the rock from which you were hewn, and to the quarry from which you were dug" (51:1). Like God who does not change, diminish, or die, the soul, too, is immortal. Thus, the Scriptures tell us, "Choose life . . . loving the LORD your God . . . holding fast to him; for that means life to you."

A swimmer in the ocean: The divine soul swimming in the ocean that is God's being cannot be distinguished from God. "Here" and "there" have merged. The frontier between "above" and "below" has been opened. Thus, we swim in God's being: "Choose life . . . loving the LORD your God . . . holding fast to him; for that means life to you."

A spark from the fire: Just as a spark is aflame like the fire from which it came, the divine soul is a spark aflame like its source which is God. Far from the fire, a spark can die. Close to the fire, the spark becomes integrated into the flame, making the spark brighter. Like sparks and the fire, we are called to: "Choose life . . . loving the LORD your God . . . holding fast to him; for that means life to you."

Caught in a welter of work, desires, conflicts, duties, and relationships, we may easily forget our divine soul, and thus miss this place of God's presence. The command to love the LORD your God should arouse the parts of our soul that are unaware of the Divine Presence within us. Since the innermost center of the soul is divine and cleaves to God, the outer parts of the soul need to be awakened to the Divine. God summons us then to "Choose life . . . loving the LORD your God . . . holding fast to him; for that means life to you."

One way of entering our innermost sanctuary is to empty the soul of all the distractions of desire and ego. The result is a vacated space that will fill with the Divine. Mystics of all ages and religious traditions have described this process using different names: for example, the *via negativa* or the *via passiva*. We offer our will, desires, hopes, and expectations to God. We listen for God's will and wait for God's grace, believing that "'unless a grain of wheat falls into the earth and dies, it remains just a single grain; but if it dies, it bears much fruit'" (John 12:24). When we die to ourself, that emptiness is filled with the fullness of God's presence.

Reflection

❏ Meditate on the reading and commentary again. Whenever a word, phrase, or sentence strikes you as particularly significant, spend time slowly repeating the words until their meaning for you becomes clear.

❏ Because God lives in our very soul, God will never leave us. Reflect on these words from Romans 8:38–39: "I am convinced that neither death, nor life, nor angels, nor rulers, nor things present, nor things to come, nor powers, nor height, nor depth, nor anything else in all creation, will be able to separate us from the love of God." Pray these words of Paul over and over. If you find writing helpful, jot down your response to these verses.

❏ God's loving desire for communication with our soul has caused Divine Life to be implanted permanently there. As a result, we are human-divine beings. Jesus came to show us that, indeed, we are human-divine, and thus, we are by God's grace associated with the nature and role of Jesus, the Messiah. Jesus calls us to be messiahs in our own time, as *filii et filiae in Filio*, or sons and daughters in the Son.

Talk to God about these questions:
- Do I believe that Divine Life is implanted in my soul?
- Am I really called to be Jesus, the Messiah, in my time?
- Have I met people who have been Jesus, another Christ, to me?
- How would my life be different if I fully assumed the role of Jesus, as Messiah, in my world?

❏ Reflect on this legend:

> There was a famous monastery which had fallen on very hard times. . . . People no longer came there to be nourished by prayer. A handful of old monks shuffled through the cloisters and praised their God with heavy hearts.

On the edge of the monastery woods, an old rabbi had built a little hut. He would come there from time to time to fast and pray. . . . And, for as long as he was there, the monks would feel sustained by his prayerful presence.

One day the abbot decided to visit the rabbi and to open his heart to him. So, after the morning Eucharist, he set out through the woods. As he approached the hut, the abbot saw the rabbi standing in the doorway, his arms outstretched in welcome. It was as though he had been waiting there for some time. The two embraced like long-lost brothers. . . .

After a while the rabbi motioned the abbot to enter. In the middle of the room was a wooden table with the Scriptures open on it. They sat there for a moment, in the presence of the Book. Then the rabbi began to cry. The abbot could not contain himself. He covered his face with his hands and began to cry too. . . . The two men sat there like lost children, filling the hut with their sobs and wetting the wood of the table with their tears.

After the tears had ceased to flow . . . the rabbi lifted his head. "You and your brothers are serving God with heavy hearts," he said. "You have come to ask a teaching of me. I will give you a teaching, but you can only repeat it once. After that, no one must ever say it aloud again."

The rabbi looked straight at the abbot and said, "The Messiah is among you.". . .

The abbot left without a word and without ever looking back.

The next morning, the abbot called his monks together in the chapter room. He told them he had received a teaching from "the rabbi who walks in the woods" and that this teaching was never again to be spoken aloud. Then he looked at each of his brothers and said, "The rabbi said that one of us is the Messiah."

The monks were startled by this saying. "What could it mean?" they asked themselves. "Is Brother John the Messiah? Or Father Matthew? . . . Am *I* the Messiah? . . ."

They were all deeply puzzled by the rabbi's teaching. But no one ever mentioned it again.

As time went by, the monks began to treat one another with a very special reverence. There was a gentle, wholehearted, human quality about them now which was hard to describe but easy to notice. They lived with one another as men who had finally found something. . . . Occasional visitors found themselves deeply moved by the life of these monks. Before long, people were coming from far and wide to be nourished by the prayer life of the monks and young men were asking, once again, to become part of the community. (Francis Dorff, "The Rabbi's Gift," *New Catholic World,* p. 53)

❑ Read the following passages from John's Gospel and ask yourself this question: How would I feel and act if I believed that Jesus were speaking these words to me?
- "'I am the light of the world'" (8:12).
- "'I will not leave you orphaned; I am coming to you'" (14:18).
- "'Very truly, I tell you, the Son can do nothing on his own, but only what he sees the Father doing; for whatever the Father does, the Son does likewise'" (5:19).

Memory Verse

Repeat this verse frequently throughout the day:

> Those of you who held fast to the LORD your God are all alive today.
>
> (Deuteronomy 4:4)

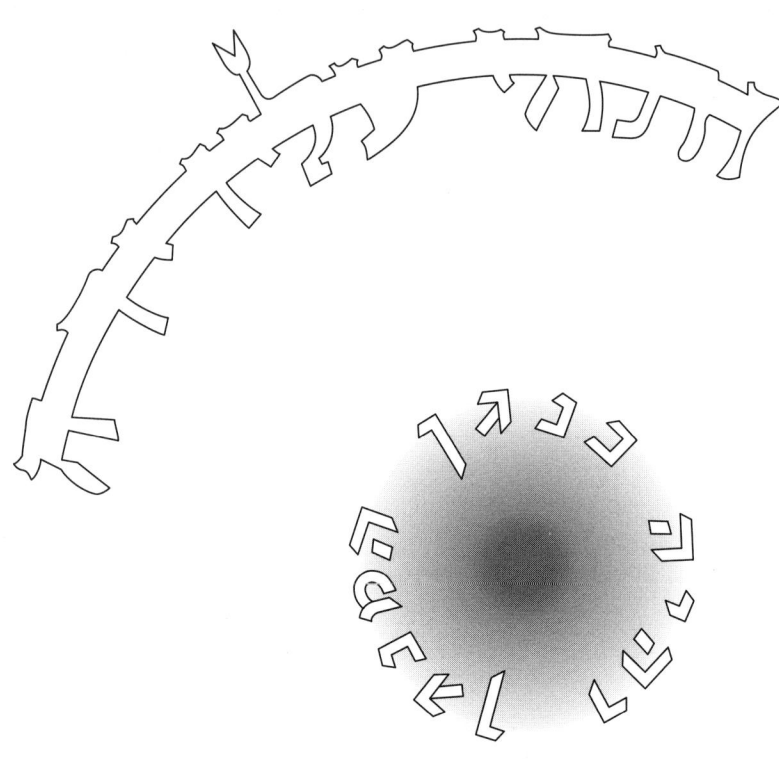

וְהָיָה כְּנַגֵּן הַמְנַגֵּן וַתְּהִי עָלָיו יַד־יְהוָה:

While the musician was playing, the power of the LORD came on him.

(2 Kings 3:15)

As the musician plays, he becomes more receptive to the Spirit of God and gradually experiences divine ecstasy. In the drawing, the dark center fades into the outer light. When the musician fades into the light, he becomes an instrument to be played by the Divine Musician. The words, "the power of the LORD came on him" are written in a single block to emphasize the power of the event. The arched words show that God shelters and envelops the musician with the Divine Spirit.

MEDITATION 10

Where is the place of God's spirit?

In the Spirit of our spirit, "While the musician was playing, the power of the LORD came on him" (2 Kings 3:15).

Introduction

We do not always have to dig for the waters of life. God sends rain. We do not always have to go in search of the Spirit of God. The Spirit is sent to us. We do not have to travel far to reach God. We are already attached to the Divine as a tree is rooted in the ground, as a stone is anchored in the quarry of God's being, and as a spark is aglow in the Divine Fire. God will also come to us when we are passive, listening, and receptive. God inspires us when we play, but also when we are played upon.

Reading

> O children of Zion, be glad
>   and rejoice in the LORD your God;
> for he has given the early rain for your vindication,
>   he has poured down for you abundant rain,
>   the early and the later rain, as before.
> The threshing floors shall be full of grain,
>   the vats shall overflow with wine and oil. . . .
>
> You shall eat in plenty and be satisfied,
>   and praise the name of the LORD your God,
>   who has dealt wondrously with you. . . .
>
> Then afterward
>   I will pour out my spirit on all flesh;

> your sons and your daughters shall prophesy,
>> your old men shall dream dreams,
>> and your young men shall see visions.
> Even on the male and female slaves,
>> in those days, I will pour out my spirit.
>
> (Joel 2:23–29)

Commentary

The fundamental posture of contemplative prayer is receptivity or hopeful waiting for God. Encountering God in contemplation comes when we silence our mouth and mind, and listen with simple attention. In contemplation, God takes the active part, while the soul becomes like a harp or a trumpet for the Divine Musician to play.

In the example of the musician, God may inspire us as we play, but the musician also serves as a model of contemplation: "While the musician was playing, the power of the LORD came on him" (2 Kings 3:15). When the musician (*ha-menaggen*) becomes like an instrument (*ke-naggen*), the power of God comes upon him.

In the Hebrew Scriptures, human souls are compared to a harp or a shofar (a ram's-horn trumpet) on which the Spirit of God plays. Unless God plays upon our soul, we make no music and have no power. God invites us to be music, to share in the divine power: "Lift up your voice like a trumpet!" (Isaiah 58:1). When we open ourselves to God in hopeful receptivity and simple attention, we are, in effect, asking that our voice be the instrument through which God speaks to the world, just like the harp, shofar, and trumpet are the instruments through which musicians make music. God's word may then pour forth from our divine soul in inspired declarations that we could never compose on our own.

During contemplation, God's spirit—the Divine Spirit already present in the human soul—moves people to visions, prophesy, and dreams. Thus, evil is crowded out of the soul. Contemplation focuses our mind on God. This focus on God is a more effective way to combat evil than one that concentrates on avoiding evil. When the Spirit enters into the receptive soul, Divine Light vanquishes evil.

God will send the Divine Spirit to our soul, and dreams and visions into our heart. In order for that to occur, we must have an open heart and a receptive spirit—in other words, we must be in the posture of contemplation.

Reflection

❏ Reflect on the reading from Joel once again. Spend time with God's words in this passage.

❏ If you have house plants or a thirsty yard, go and water them. Concentrate on what you are doing; imagine the water seeping into the ground and into the roots. Recall that you water your plants or yard because you care for them. The plants do not ask to be watered. They depend on you. God sends rain, not because God has to, but out of care. Thank God for the rain on which you depend and for which all you can do is hope, wait, and be ready with buckets and tilled soil.

❏ If you play a musical instrument, play a favorite song on it, offering the song to God. If you wish, sing, whistle, or hum a hymn with your own bodily instrument. Then slowly and repeatedly pray: Come upon me and open my lips, O God, that I may be an instrument for your word.

❏ "'Whenever you pray, go into your room and shut the door and pray to your Father who is in secret; and your Father who sees in secret will reward you'" (Matthew 6:6). The temple of your soul is your prayer room. Quiet your mind by closing your eyes and breathing deeply and slowly. Quiet your body by stretching each part of it, starting with your feet. When you are relaxed, begin praying one word in rhythm with your breathing: as you inhale, speak the word *Spirit, Jesus,* or another holy name; repeat the word as you exhale. If a distracting thought or feeling flits into your mind, just let it go, repeating the sacred name once again. After a while, you may cease speaking the name. Then you can sit attentively, waiting for God's spirit. Rest receptively with God.
    Close by praying several times: "'The Mighty One has done great things for me'" (Luke 1:49).

❑ If you have an issue in your life that darkens your spirit and stifles your song—an issue you seem to lack control over—offer it to God. Admit your powerlessness and ask God to open your heart to receive whatever grace you need. Pray to be receptive to God's power.

Memory Verse

Whenever you hear music today, recall and pray these words:

> While the musician was playing, the power of the LORD came on him.
>
> (2 Kings 3:15)

ה מְחַיֶּה מֵתִים בְּרַחֲמִים רַבִּים

Thou . . . revivest the dead with great mercy.
(Birnbaum, *Daily Prayer Book*, p. 84)

God's abundant mercy reaches even into death. Nothing can tarnish God's glory, symbolized by the wreath of beams formed from the shining letters. At the same time, this circle is like a hand that pulls the dead person out of the darkness of death into the light of heaven. The process of resurrection is seen in the transformation of the letters of the word מתים, *death. On the side of death, the letters are still black; on the side of eternal life, they are light and shining like the letters that compose the circle of God.*

MEDITATION 11

Where is God's place in our dying?

In the very midst of death, "Thou . . . revivest the dead with great mercy" (Birnbaum, *Daily Prayer Book*, p. 84).

Introduction

Our hearts are restless for God. Like a dry and weary land without water, we long for God. But where do we look for God? In no other place is God considered so powerfully and mercifully present as in our dying and death. When we say, "we are drawing nearer to death," we also mean, "we are drawing nearer to God."

Reading

> Thou, O Lord, art mighty forever; thou revivest the dead; thou art powerful to save.
> Thou causest the wind to blow and the rain to fall.
> Thou sustainest the living with kindness, and revivest the dead with great mercy; thou supportest all who fall, and healest the sick; thou settest the captives free, and keepest faith with those who sleep in the dust. Who is like thee, Lord of power? Who resembles thee, O King? Thou bringest death and restorest life, and causest salvation to flourish. . . .
> Thou art faithful to revive the dead. Blessed art thou, O Lord, who revivest the dead. (Birnbaum, *Daily Prayer Book*, p. 84)

Commentary

God is powerfully and mercifully present to those who die. In the reading above, God's power and mercy receive special emphasis.

God's power: God's position of great power is named *Ha-Gevurah,* meaning "the All Powerful One." At significant moments, the All Powerful One speaks. Moses received the Ten Commandments from the mouth of the All Powerful One. Jesus spoke "as one having authority" (Mark 1:22), as the *Ha-Gevurah,* meaning that he taught the people as one who spoke the very words issued from the mouth of God and not as one who repeated the statements of others. When the dead are revived, they are revived by the word that comes from the mouth of the All Powerful One.

God's mercy: With God's power comes God's abundant mercy. Loving kindness sustains the living, and abundant mercy protects the dead: "Thou . . . revivest the dead with great mercy." With abundant mercy God causes death but restores life.

In the Jewish prayer, two natural images speak to us of God's presence in our death and resurrection: the awaking from sleep and the revival of the earth through the falling rain.

Death is presented as a kind of sleep. When we sleep, we lie nestled in the arms of God who re-creates us during the hours of rest just as jewellers renew and polish jewels left in their keeping. When we wake from sleep, it is as if we are waking from death. God dwells with us in our sleep and in our death. Renewed and restored to life, we pray, "I render thanks to thee, everlasting King, who hast mercifully restored my soul within me; thy faithfulness is great" (Birnbaum, *Daily Prayer Book,* p. 2).

Rain revivifies the parched earth, causing that which was dry and dormant to sprout forth new life. As rain brings life out of the earth, so does the All Powerful One revive the dead: God, "restorest life and causest salvation to flourish." The words, "Thou causest the wind to blow and the rain to fall" serve to remind us of revival of the dead through the power and mercy of the ever-present God.

In our death and resurrection, the temple of our spirit that houses the Divine is renewed and transformed so that we see

> "What no eye has seen, nor ear heard,
> nor the human heart conceived."
>
> (1 Corinthians 2:9)

Reflection

❏ Pray the reading slowly and meditatively.

❏ Bring to mind the death of a close friend, parent, or someone else you loved. Ponder the following questions:
- What feelings filled you as you thought about the death?
- Where did you receive consolation?
- Have you been able to let go of your grief?
- Considering the death of this special person, does the reading provide consolation, or does it seem ironic?

❏ Unfortunately, a parent with a life-threatening illness has to explain the likelihood of his or her own death to children in the family. The prospect of such a conversation is wrenching. Imagine that you have to prepare yourself and a loved one for your own death. What will you say about your own death? Write down how you will discuss the meaning of your life and death. Then imagine that you, your loved one, and Jesus are seated together. Speak to them the words you have written. Let them speak to you in response. What will they tell you? Close your talk by praying the words of the reading.

❏ Meditate on the wonder of rain falling on the dry earth. If it helps, close your eyes and imagine a spring rain falling on freshly tilled and planted soil. Hear and smell the rain. Imagine the earth soaking in the life-giving water and the seeds sprouting. Then see the tiny gold-green stems peeking out of the earth. Let your imagination dwell lovingly on these images. When you feel ready, pray: Praise to you, God who sends the rain. Just so, you revive the dead and cause salvation to sprout.

❏ Tonight when you prepare for sleep, offer God this prayer: You keep faith with those who sleep.

Tomorrow morning when you wake up, thank God that you have been renewed and revitalized during your sleep: I render thanks to you, everlasting One who has mercifully restored my soul within me; your faithfulness is great.

❏ Reflect on these words of Saint Paul and imagine what the afterlife may be like: "For now we see in a mirror, dimly, but then we will see face to face. Now I know only in part; then I will know fully, even as I have been fully known" (1 Corinthians 13:12).

❏ Sing a favorite hymn that celebrates the Resurrection and its promise or that declares your deep faith in God's abundant mercy—for example, any version of the Twenty-third Psalm, "Amazing Grace," or "How Can I Keep from Singing?"

Memory Verse

Visit the graves of loved ones. Thank God for these special people. At each grave, pray this verse:

> Thou . . . revivest the dead with great mercy.
> (Birnbaum, *Daily Prayer Book,* p. 84)

For Further Reading

Meditation 1

Freedman, H., and Maurice Simon, eds. and trans. *Midrash Rabbah.* Vol. 1. New York: Soncino Press, 1977. See pages 8–9.

Meditation 4

Freedman, H., and Maurice Simon, eds. and trans. *Midrash Rabbah.* Vol. 2. New York: Soncino Press, 1977. See pages 52–53.

Meditation 5

Encyclopaedia Judaica, s.v. "Kiddush Ha-Shem and Hillul Ha-Shem."
Peli, Pinchas H. *On Repentance: In the Thought and Oral Discourses of Rabbi Joseph B. Soloveitchik.* Jerusalem: Oroth Publishing House. See pages 93–97 and 216–224.

Meditation 9

Baer, Dobh. *On Ecstasy.* Translated by Louis Jacobs. Chappaqua, NY: Rossel Books, 1963. See page 66.
Jacobs, Louis. *A Jewish Theology.* New York: Behrman House, 1973. See pages 35–37 and 63.

Meditation 10

Guyon, Jeanne. *Experiencing the Depths of Jesus Christ.* Gardiner, ME: Christian Books, 1975. See page 12.

Jacobs, Louis. *Hasidic Prayer*. New York: Schocken Books, 1972. See pages 99–100.

Meditation 11

Cohen, A. *Everyman's Talmud*. New York: E. P. Dutton, 1932. See page 381.

Urbach, Ephraim E. *The Sages: Their Concepts and Beliefs*. Jerusalem: Magnes Press, 1975. See page 85.

Acknowledgments (continued)

The scriptural quotations used in this book are from the New Revised Standard Version of the Bible. Copyright © 1989 by the Division of Christian Education of the National Council of the Churches of Christ in the United States of America. Used with permission.

The first excerpt on page 6 is from the poem "God's Grandeur," by Gerard Manley Hopkins in *Poems of Gerard Manley Hopkins*, 3d ed., edited by W. H. Gardner (New York and London: Oxford University Press, 1948), page 70.

The second excerpt on page 6 is from *Tales of the Hasidim: The Early Masters*, by Martin Buber (New York: Schocken Books, 1947), page 212.

The excerpt on page 10 is used as quoted in *Seminary Education and Christian-Jewish Relations: A Curriculum and Resource Handbook*, by Eugene J. Fisher (Washington, DC: The National Catholic Educational Association Seminary Department, 1983), appendix D.

The excerpt on page 37 is from *The Midrash Rabbah*, vol. 2, translated by H. Freedman and Maurice Simon (London: Soncino Press, 1977), page 53.

The excerpts on pages 47–48 and 53 are from *Prayer Book for Sabbath and Festivals*, translated by Philip Birnbaum (New York: Hebrew Publishing Company, 1978), page 148. Copyright © 1978 by Philip Birnbaum.

The excerpts on pages 49–50; 51–52; 65–66; 85 and 86; 87; and 89 are from *Daily Prayer Book: Ha-Siddur Ha-Shalem*, translated by Philip Birnbaum (New York: Hebrew Publishing Company, 1977), pages 84 and 86; 50; 74 and 76; 84; 2; and 84, respectively. Reprinted by permission of the publishers, Hebrew Publishing Company, P.O. Box 157, Rockaway Beach, NY 11693. Copyright © 1977. All rights reserved.

The excerpt on page 52 is from *The Spiritual Exercises of St. Ignatius*, translated by David L. Fleming (Saint Louis, MO: The Institute of Jesuit Sources, 1978), page 141.

The excerpt on page 57 is from *The Zohar*, vol. 5, translated by Maurice Simon and Harry Sperling (London: Soncino Press, 1949), page 211.

The excerpt on pages 57–58 is from *The Zohar,* vol. 3, translated by Harry Sperling, Maurice Simon, and Paul P. Levertoff (London: Soncino Press, 1949), pages 301–302.

The excerpt on page 66 is from *The Mishnah,* translated by Herbert Danby (London: Oxford University Press, 1933), pages 10–11.

The excerpt on pages 75–77 is from "The Rabbi's Gift," by Francis Dorff, which appeared in *New Catholic World* 222 (March–April 1979): 53. Used with permission.